TODAY'S SPORTS GREATS

DWYANE WADE

By Jason Glaser

Gareth Stevens
Publishing

Please visit our website, www.garethstevens.com. For a free color catalog of all our high-quality books, call toll free 1-800-542-2595 or fax 1-877-542-2596.

Library of Congress Cataloging-in-Publication Data

Glaser, Jason.
Dwyane Wade / Jason Glaser.
     p. cm. — (Today's sports greats)
Includes index.
ISBN 978-1-4339-5864-9 (pbk.)
ISBN 978-1-4339-5865-6 (6-pack)
ISBN 978-1-4339-5862-5 (library binding)
1. Wade, Dwyane, 1982- 2. Basketball players—United States—Biography. I. Title.
GV884.W23G53 2011
796.323092—dc22
[B]

                                  2010048163

First Edition

Published in 2012 by
Gareth Stevens Publishing
111 East 14th Street, Suite 349
New York, NY 10003

Copyright © 2012 Gareth Stevens Publishing

Designer: Michael J. Flynn
Editor: Therese Shea

Photo credits: Cover, p. 1 Eliot J. Schechter/Getty Images; cover, pp. 2–32, back cover (stadium background), 4–5 (skyline) Shutterstock.com; p. 4 (Wade) Jeffery A. Salter/ Sports Illustrated/Getty Images; pp. 6, 27 Walter Iooss Jr./Sports Illustrated/Getty Images; p. 7 Rick Stewart/Getty Images; p. 9 Andy Lyons/Getty Images; pp. 10–11 John Biever/ Sports Illustrated/Getty Images; p. 13 (Wade) Todd Rosenberg/Sports Illustrated/ Getty Images; p. 13 (Riley) Kevin C. Cox/Getty Images; p. 14 Jeff Gross/Getty Images; p. 15 Matt Stroshane/Getty Images; pp. 16, 20 Doug Benc/Getty Images; p. 17 Brian Bahr/ Getty Images; p. 19 (Wade) Ronald Martinez/Getty Images; p. 19 (Mourning) Jim McIsaac/ Getty Images; p. 21 Jonathan Daniel/Getty Images; p. 22 Jim Rogash/Getty Images; p. 23 Marc Serota/Getty Images; p. 24 Elsa/Getty Images; p. 25 Alexander Tamargo/ WireImage/Getty Images; p. 26 Saul Loeb/AFP/Getty Images; p. 29 Mike Ehrmann/ Getty Images.

Printed in the United States of America

CPSIA compliance information: Batch #CS11GS: For further information contact Gareth Stevens, New York, New York at 1-800-542-2595.

CONTENTS

Words in the glossary appear in **bold** type the first time they are used in the text.

A SISTER'S LOVE

Now a role model himself, basketball star Dwyane Wade's first role model was his older sister Tragil. Their parents separated shortly after Dwyane was born. They lived with their mother and two stepsisters on Chicago's South Side. Tragil was 5 years older than Dwyane—and he followed her everywhere! He admired her self-confidence and was grateful to her for taking care of him. Their mother couldn't because she was battling drug and alcohol addictions.

Dwyane Wade was born on January 17, 1982. Chicago's South Side, shown here, was his first home.

When Dwyane was 8, Tragil did the hardest thing a caring sister could do: she sent him away. Dwyane went to live with their father so that he could grow up in a safer neighborhood, away from gangs and drugs. He could also grow up among male relatives, including three stepbrothers.

The Pride of Robbins, Illinois

Dwyane's father moved the family to Robbins, Illinois. It's a small town south of Chicago. Robbins is proud of more than basketball superstar Dwyane Wade. It was home to a small airport that was once the only place African Americans could learn to become pilots. This place helped prepare pilots for a military training program in Tuskegee, Alabama. The Tuskegee Airmen were a heroic group of highly successful World War II fighter pilots.

DID YOU KNOW?

Dwyane Wade's full name is Dwyane Tyrone Wade Jr. He's named after his father.

THE FAMILY TRADITION

Like many young men in and around Chicago, Dwyane loved basketball. His father coached a youth team, and his brothers played as well. Many days, the Wade family played against each other outside their home until long after sunset. Dwyane's father and older brothers didn't take it easy on him, making him earn every shot he made through the wooden hoop.

Dwyane's older sister Tragil poses here with their father Dwyane Wade Sr.

DID YOU KNOW?

Dwyane played basketball with many neighborhood kids. One—Siohvaughn Funches—became his friend, then his girlfriend, and eventually his wife.

One of Dwyane's stepbrothers, Demetris, was a star on the high school basketball team. When Dwyane was in eighth grade, Demetris asked the coach to let Dwyane practice with the team. Dwyane wasn't a great player at this point. However, just an hour of watching Dwyane **dribble** around impressed the coach. He saw a future star.

Michael Jordan

At the time Wade was growing up, Chicago was the center of the basketball universe. The Chicago Bulls won six NBA (National Basketball Association) championships during the 1990s, due mainly to a superstar named Michael Jordan. Jordan was an inspiration to millions of young fans and ballplayers like Wade. He was dazzlingly quick and a sure shot. Wade has said that he **idolized** Jordan and modeled his game after the superstar's. Wade also became a **shooting guard** just like Jordan.

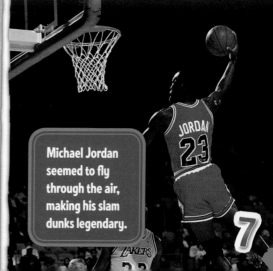

Michael Jordan seemed to fly through the air, making his slam dunks legendary.

OLD SCHOOL, NEW SCHOOL

Wade wasn't a key part of his high school team during his first 2 years. He had trouble scoring and didn't play a lot. By his junior year, though, he had practiced enough to become a better shooter and dribbler. He also grew 4 inches (10 cm) by his senior year! Suddenly Wade was scoring points, blocking shots, and winning games.

Despite Wade's on-court success, few colleges paid attention to him. His grades and test scores were too low to allow him to get into many schools with basketball programs. Even so, the coach at Marquette University in Wisconsin saw something special in Wade and wanted him on the team. With the condition that he wouldn't play until his grades improved, Wade received Marquette's first **conditional** scholarship.

DID YOU KNOW?

The basketball court at H. L. Richards High School is officially named "D Wade Court" after Wade gave the school money to build a new gymnasium.

Dwyane Wade's High School Career

Wade played for H. L. Richards High School in Oak Lawn, Illinois, a school with a strong basketball history. The school has had many good players, but Wade is among the best. He's the only Richards player ever to reach the school's all-time top five in scoring, **assists**, **rebounds**, steals, and **blocks**. With Wade's help, the school achieved both **conference** and regional championships in his junior and senior years.

Wade drives hard to the basket for the Marquette University Golden Eagles.

Although Wade couldn't play as a college freshman, he was still an important member of the team. In practice, he took the role of the opposing team's best player so Marquette could work on defense. During home games, he studied his teammates and made notes on how they could play better. This work paid off for Wade as well. His grades improved, and he was allowed to play the following year. By then, he'd become skilled in basketball **strategy**.

On the court, Wade quickly made his mark. He scored more points than any other sophomore in school history. As a junior, he helped Marquette make it to the Final Four of the NCAA (National Collegiate Athletic Association) tournament for the first time since 1977.

DID YOU KNOW?

With an average score of 19.7 points per game, Wade has the second-highest per game average in Marquette history.

Triple Double

During the 2003 NCAA tournament, Wade accomplished a difficult basketball feat to get Marquette to the Final Four. It's called a "triple double." A triple double occurs when a player gets 10 or more in three of the following categories: points, rebounds, assists, steals, and blocks. In the game against the University of Kentucky, Wade got 29 points, 11 rebounds, and 11 assists, and led his team to victory.

Wade was named the Conference USA Player of the Year for the 2002–2003 season.

Wade's performance in the NCAA tournament caught the interest of television and newspaper reporters as well as several NBA teams. With all the attention, Wade felt it was a good time to enter the NBA **draft**. This meant leaving college before his senior year. By this time, however, Wade was already married and had a son, Zaire. An NBA contract would bring in lots of money to take care of his young family.

The 2003 draft was one of the strongest in NBA history. It featured players such as LeBron James, Carmelo Anthony, and Chris Bosh. Even so, Wade was picked fifth overall, the highest ever for a Marquette player. He would be playing for the Miami Heat.

DID YOU KNOW?

Wade's nicknames are "Flash" and "D. Wade."

Pat Riley and the Miami Heat

The key person responsible for bringing Wade to Miami was Pat Riley, who was the team's coach and general manager. At the time, Miami had missed the playoffs the previous 2 years after having made them 6 years straight under Riley. The Heat had played so badly in 2002–2003 that Riley announced he was going to "fire himself" as coach. He stepped down at the beginning of the following season.

Wade has continued using his college number, 3, in the pros.

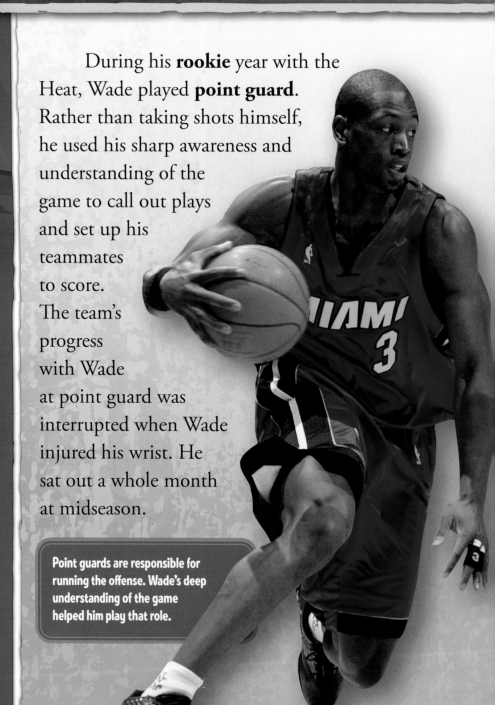

During his **rookie** year with the Heat, Wade played **point guard**. Rather than taking shots himself, he used his sharp awareness and understanding of the game to call out plays and set up his teammates to score. The team's progress with Wade at point guard was interrupted when Wade injured his wrist. He sat out a whole month at midseason.

Point guards are responsible for running the offense. Wade's deep understanding of the game helped him play that role.

During the second half of the season, the Heat ignited. Wade began lighting up the scoreboard. He scored double digits in 51 games and set a Heat rookie record for the number of **field goals** in a single game with 15. The Heat made it to the playoffs. The team only got as far as the second round that year, but the rookie gave them hope for future success.

Disappointment on the World Stage

Following his rookie season, Wade played on the 2004 Olympic team. Since 1992, when professional players were first allowed to play in the Olympics, the United States had never lost a basketball game. Yet, even with Wade and the immense talent on the team, the United States lost three games before winning the bronze medal instead of the gold. The failure was bitter for Wade, but it motivated him to help lead the "Redeem Team" of 2008 back to gold-medal glory.

SO CLOSE, YET SO FAR

With youth on their side, the Miami Heat paired Wade with some "big" experience after a trade for NBA legend Shaquille O'Neal. Now back to shooting guard, Wade worked the outside while O'Neal played near the basket. Wade nearly doubled his point total from the previous season and became the team's leading scorer.

O'Neal and Wade were an exciting duo to watch. O'Neal stayed in Miami until 2008.

DID YOU KNOW?

The 2004–2005 season brought Wade his first invitation to play in the All-Star game.

A Thorn in His Side

During the fifth game of the 2005 conference finals, with the series tied at two games per team, Wade pulled a muscle near his ribs. He was forced to leave the game when the pain worsened. The Heat had a large lead and still won that game. The injury kept Wade out of game six, and the Heat lost. Trying to save the series, Wade returned for the final game but couldn't play his best. The Heat lost the game, the series, and their chance at the NBA Finals.

In the 2005 playoffs, Wade took his game to an even higher level, playing over 40 minutes per game and averaging over 27 points. He led the team in points, assists, and steals. The Heat met the Detroit Pistons in the conference championship series. Although the Heat took a 3–2 lead in the series, the Pistons came through to win the finals in game seven.

More determined than ever, Wade scored over 2,000 points on the path to the 2006 playoffs. Once again, the Heat faced the Pistons in the conference finals. When Wade suffered a flu-like illness, Heat fans feared the worst. Amazingly, Wade powered through and got revenge on the Pistons. The Heat moved on to the NBA Finals.

At first, the Dallas Mavericks seemed too strong to defeat, winning two games and leading in the third. However, Wade answered with a burst of scoring—42 points in all! He didn't slow down until the Heat had won the NBA championship. For his high-scoring games and leadership, Wade was named Finals MVP (Most Valuable Player). His performance is regarded as one of the best in finals history.

DID YOU KNOW?

Dwyane Wade became the first of the 2003 draft's first-round picks to lead his team to a title.

Dwyane Wade became the fifth-youngest NBA Finals MVP.

Alonzo Mourning

In 2005, the Heat welcomed back NBA star Alonzo Mourning. Mourning had been suffering from kidney disease, but a kidney **transplant** let him have one more run for the NBA title. The fan favorite became a teacher and friend to Wade, guiding him to become one of the best players in the game. Wade went on to pass Mourning as the leading scorer in Miami Heat history.

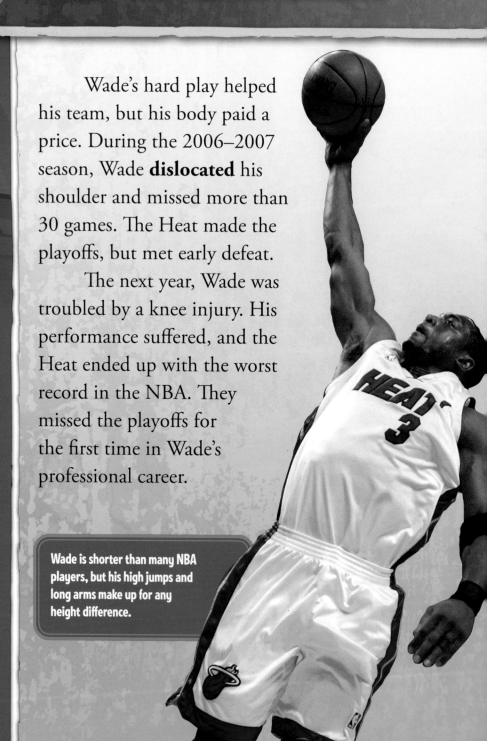

THE ROAD BACK

Wade's hard play helped his team, but his body paid a price. During the 2006–2007 season, Wade **dislocated** his shoulder and missed more than 30 games. The Heat made the playoffs, but met early defeat.

The next year, Wade was troubled by a knee injury. His performance suffered, and the Heat ended up with the worst record in the NBA. They missed the playoffs for the first time in Wade's professional career.

Wade is shorter than many NBA players, but his high jumps and long arms make up for any height difference.

In the 2008–2009 season, Heat fans breathed a sigh of relief. Wade played healthy for the whole year. It showed—he was the league's top scorer with 2,386 points! The Heat returned to the playoffs, but suffered a disappointing loss in the first round.

Marquette Honors Dwyane

Marquette University admitted Wade on a scholarship despite his poor academic record, and it paid off with a trip to the Final Four. The school bent the rules once more when they retired his jersey number in 2007. Usually, a former student must have graduated in order to receive this honor. Wade had left the university after his junior year to enter the NBA. However, Wade's NBA championship and superstar skills were more than enough to convince Marquette to extend the honor to him.

DID YOU KNOW?

In the 2008–2009 season, Wade recorded over 2,000 points, 500 assists, 100 steals, and 100 blocks. He's the only player in NBA history to reach those numbers in one season.

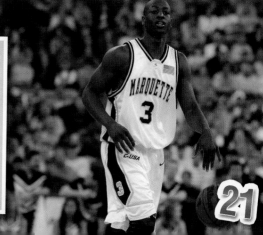

THE GANG'S ALL HERE

The 2009–2010 season was successful for Dwyane Wade. He scored over 2,000 points and was the team's leading scorer in 62 of the 77 games he played. Still, the Heat was beaten early in the playoffs. Wade could carry his team a long way, but only so far.

LeBron James

Chris Bosh

Dwyane Wade

By staying in Miami and convincing stars LeBron James and Chris Bosh to join him, Wade made the Heat an immediate favorite to win the championship.

Through rookie events, the Olympics, and All-Star games, Wade had become friends with LeBron James and other top 2003 rookies. Many were becoming free agents, meaning they could sign with new teams. In a move that shocked the league, Wade helped convince James and friendly rival Chris Bosh to come to Miami. The Heat became perhaps the most talented team the NBA had seen in recent years.

DID YOU KNOW?

Early in the 2009-2010 season, Wade became the first Heat player to score 10,000 points with the team.

The Injury Bug

Once LeBron James and Chris Bosh signed with the Heat, many sports observers felt that injuries were the only thing that could stop the Heat. Wade had spent time off the court due to illness and injury in previous years, as had Bosh. This grim forecast came true as Wade and James suffered leg injuries early in the season.

FAMILY TIES

Wade's childhood gave him a special perspective on family life. He is thankful for his family and knows his sons—Zaire and Zion—need a better life than the one he had as a boy. Wade's wealth has kept his children in a safe, comfortable home, but there are still similarities. Like his parents before him, Wade and his wife divorced. Like young Dwyane, Wade's sons will be watched over by their mother most of the time. Even when Wade is caring for Zaire and Zion, his sister watches the boys when he travels for games.

Wade and son Zaire watch the Los Angeles Lakers take on the Boston Celtics in the 2010 NBA Finals.

Jolinda Wade

Where Is Dwyane Wade's Home?

It's hard to tell where Wade calls home. He identifies Robbins as his hometown, but has deep connections to Chicago and owns a home there. He spends long stretches in Miami during the basketball season. In 2010, Wade sold his Florida house and now lives in a Miami luxury apartment. When he's not in any of these places, he's vacationing, on the road for games, or traveling for photo shoots, appearances, and charity events.

Wade's mother is now a part of his life again. Motivated to be a bigger part of her family's life, Jolinda Wade beat her addictions, straightened out her life, and became a preacher.

DID YOU KNOW?

To help his mother, Wade bought her not just a house and car in Chicago, but also her own church.

25

GIVING BACK

Wade's fortune has led him to want to help others. He created a charity organization called Wade's World to help kids in at-risk situations accomplish their dreams. He attends charity events and fundraisers that work to stop gang violence. He has helped a Robbins public library stay open. He has also aided a Miami family in buying a new home after their house burned down. Wade visits children's hospitals with jerseys and signed basketballs for young patients.

Wade's leadership earned him a meeting with another famous former Chicago resident: President Barack Obama.

Wade's generous and genuine efforts to help others earned him the title of *Sports Illustrated's* 2006 Sportsman of the Year. Some people say that nice guys finish last. Clearly Wade is willing to take that risk as he works toward more success in the future.

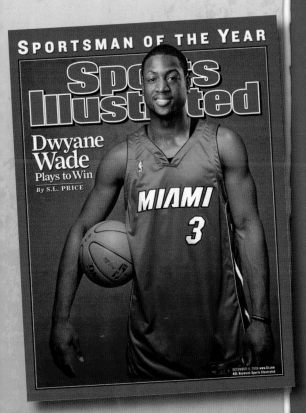

SPORTSMAN OF THE YEAR

Sports Illustrated

Dwyane Wade Plays to Win
By S.L. PRICE

MIAMI 3

A Hero's Welcome

Not many people get a chance to meet their sports heroes. Even fewer get chosen to step into their hero's shoes. Wade got to do that in real life. Michael Jordan picked him to be the new face of his "Air Jordan" line of sneakers in television commercials and print ads. Wade is the only person other than Jordan himself to represent these world-famous shoes.

DID YOU KNOW?

Dwyane Wade says that he gives one-tenth of his pay to his church. In 2010, that would have been over $1 million!

27

WHAT MAKES WADE A STAR?

Some might wonder what makes Dwyane Wade a star. How is he different from any other NBA player? At 6 feet 4 inches (193 cm), he's shorter than many players on the court. However, Wade plays a physical, **aggressive** style of basketball. He either muscles his way to the basket or quickly shifts to an open spot for a clear shot. Wade matches up against big players with his ability to leap high to dunk and block. Being smaller has its advantages, too. It allows Wade to crouch and steal balls from taller opponents.

Dwyane Wade's playing style developed as a youth practicing against his father and stepbrothers. He learned to fight toward the basket against bigger opponents. Wade continues to fight for championships as one of today's sports greats.

DID YOU KNOW?

In the 2008–2009 season, Wade became the first player under 6 feet 5 inches (196 cm) to block 100 shots in a single season.

Dwyane Wade's NBA Numbers

Season	Field Goals	Three-Pointers	Free Throws	Rebounds	Assists	Steals	Blocks
2003–2004	371	16	233 (75%)	247	275	86	34
2004–2005	630	13	581 (76%)	397	520	121	82
2005–2006	699	13	629 (78%)	430	503	146	58
2006–2007	472	21	432 (81%)	239	384	107	62
2007–2008	439	22	354 (76%)	214	354	87	37
2008–2009	854	88	590 (77%)	398	589	173	106
2009–2010	719	73	534 (76%)	373	501	142	82
Total	**4,184**	**246**	**3,353 (77%)**	**2,298**	**3,126**	**862**	**461**

GLOSSARY

aggressive: acting with forceful energy and determination

assist: a pass from one player to another that allows the second player to score

block: the act of stopping a shot from reaching the basket without touching the shot taker

conditional: describing something that will happen only if something else happens

conference: a group of sports teams that compete with each other

dislocate: to move out of its usual place within the body due to a blow or strain

draft: the selection of new players for a team

dribble: to move a ball on a basketball court by bouncing it with one hand

field goal: a score other than a free throw, worth two or three points depending on the distance from the basket

idolize: to admire greatly

point guard: the player who is responsible for directing a team's offensive play

rebound: to get the ball after it bounces off the backboard or rim of the net

rookie: a player who is in the first year of playing a sport

shooting guard: a player known for scoring and ball handling

strategy: a plan of action to achieve a goal

transplant: a medical procedure in which an organ is taken from one person and placed within another

Books

Keith, Ted. *Dwyane Wade*. Mankato, MN: Child's World, 2008.

Smithwick, John. *Meet Dwyane Wade: Basketball's Rising Star*. New York, NY: PowerKids Press, 2007.

Young, Jeff C. *Dwyane Wade*. Philadelphia, PA: Mason Crest Publishers, 2009.

Websites

Heat
www.nba.com/heat/
Check out the official news and numbers of the Miami Heat throughout the NBA basketball season.

The Official Site: DwyaneWade.com
www.dwyanewade3.com
Read Dwyane Wade's blog, and explore news articles and videos of Wade's games and appearances.

INDEX